S0-AAE-865

Exploring the Galaxy

Jupiter

by Thomas K. Adamson

Consulting Editor: Gail Saunders-Smith, PhD

Consultant: James Gerard
Aerospace Education Specialist, NASA
Kennedy Space Center, Florida

Capstone press

Mankato, Minnesota

Pebble Plus is published by Capstone Press,
151 Good Counsel Drive, P.O. Box 669, Mankato, Minnesota 56002.
www.capstonepress.com

Copyright © 2008 by Capstone Press, a Coughlan Publishing Company. All rights reserved.
No part of this publication may be reproduced in whole or in part, or stored in a retrieval system, or transmitted in any form
or by any means, electronic, mechanical, photocopying, recording, or otherwise, without written permission of the publisher.
For information regarding permission, write to Capstone Press,
151 Good Counsel Drive, P.O. Box 669, Dept. R, Mankato, Minnesota 56002.
Printed in the United States of America

1 2 3 4 5 6 12 11 10 09 08 07

Library of Congress Cataloging-in-Publication Data
Adamson, Thomas K., 1970–
     Jupiter / by Thomas K. Adamson.—Rev. and updated.
     p. cm.—(Pebble plus. Exploring the galaxy)
     Includes bibliographical references and index.
     ISBN-13: 978-1-4296-0738-4 (hardcover)
     ISBN-10: 1-4296-0738-6 (hardcover)
     1. Jupiter (Planet)—Juvenile literature. I. Title. II. Series.
QB661.A33 2008
523.45—dc22   2007004451

Summary: Simple text and photographs describe the planet Jupiter.

Editorial Credits
Mari C. Schuh, editor; Kia Adams, designer; Alta Schaffer, photo researcher

Photo Credits
Digital Vision, 5 (Venus)
John Foster/Photo Researchers, 20–21
NASA, 1, 9, 11, 12–13, 15 (Jupiter), 17, 19; JPL, 5 (Jupiter); JPL/Caltech, 5 (Uranus)
PhotoDisc, Inc., cover, 4 (Neptune), 5 (Earth, Sun, Saturn, Mars, and Mercury), 15 (Earth)
Photri-Microstock/NASA, 6–7

Note to Parents and Teachers

The Exploring the Galaxy set supports national science standards related to earth science. This book describes and illustrates the planet Jupiter. The photographs support early readers in understanding the text. The repetition of words and phrases helps early readers learn new words. This book also introduces early readers to subject-specific vocabulary words, which are defined in the Glossary section. Early readers may need assistance to read some words and to use the Table of Contents, Glossary, Read More, Internet Sites, and Index sections of the book.

Table of Contents

The Largest Planet

Jupiter is the fifth planet
from the Sun.
Jupiter is the largest planet
in the solar system.

The Solar System

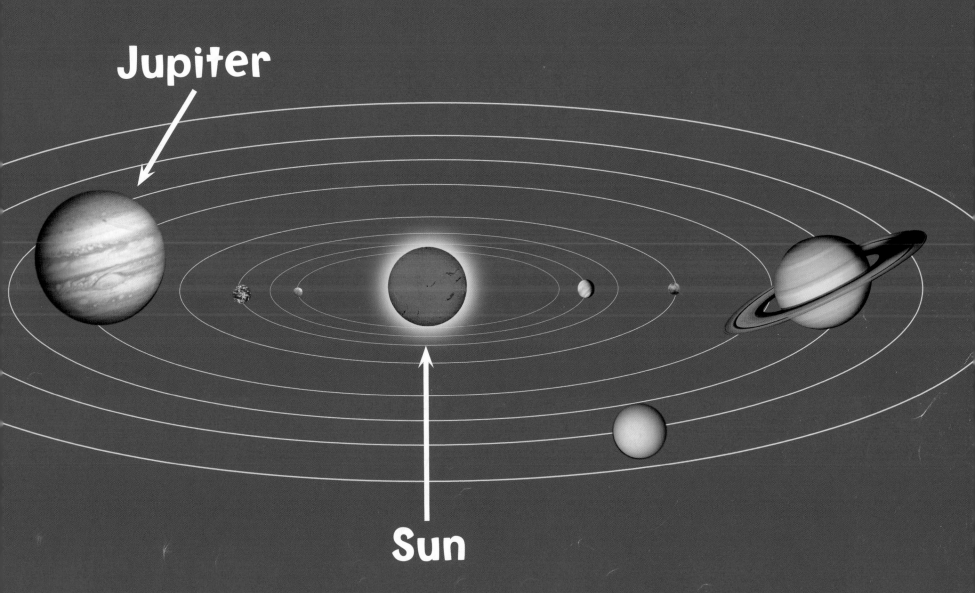

Jupiter

Sun

Jupiter is made
mostly of gases.
It is called
a gas giant.

7

Jupiter's Surface

Jupiter has no solid surface.

A spacecraft cannot

land on Jupiter.

But it can study

Jupiter's gases up close.

9

Orange and white clouds
circle Jupiter.
The clouds are thick.

The Great Red Spot

is a large storm on Jupiter.

The storm is twice

as big as Earth.

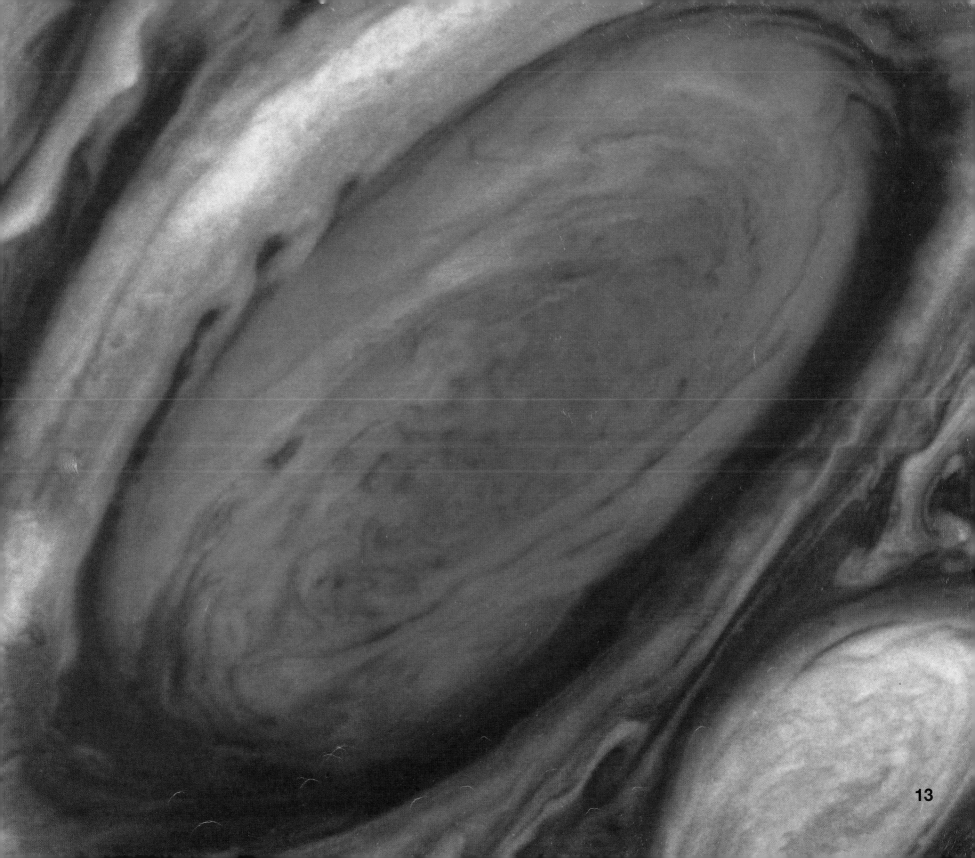

13

Size and Moons

Jupiter is much bigger
than Earth.
Jupiter is bigger
than all of the other planets
put together.

Earth

Jupiter has at least 47 moons.

Earth has only one moon.

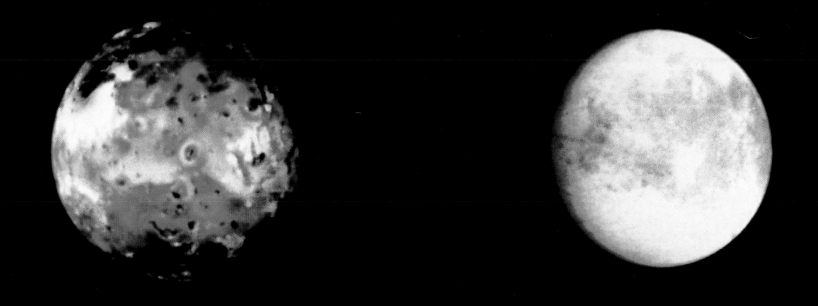

four of Jupiter's moons

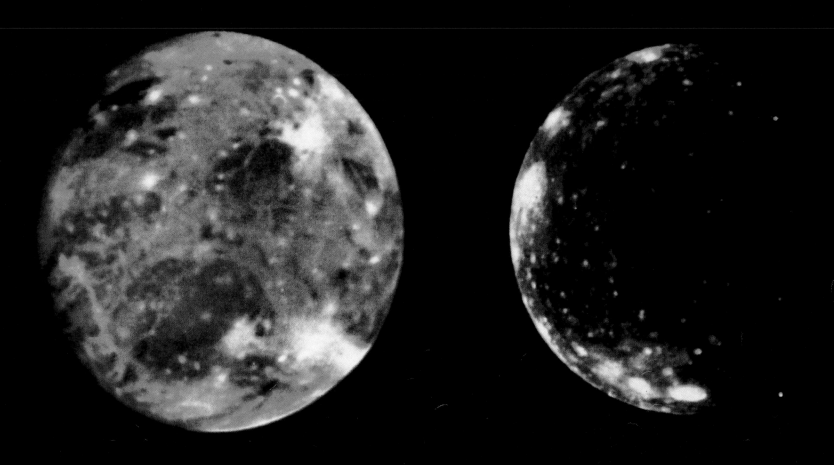

People and Jupiter

People could not breathe

the air on Jupiter.

Most of the air is very thick.

People can see Jupiter

from Earth.

Jupiter looks like

a bright star.

Jupiter

Glossary

breathe—to take air in and out of the lungs; people and animals must breathe to live.

gas—a substance, such as air, that spreads to fill any space that holds it; Jupiter is made mostly of gases.

moon—an object that moves around a planet; Io, Europa, Ganymede, and Callisto are Jupiter's largest moons.

planet—a large object that moves around the Sun; Jupiter is the fifth planet from the Sun; there are eight planets in the solar system.

solar system—the Sun and the objects that move around it; our solar system has eight planets, dwarf planets including Pluto, and many moons, asteroids, and comets.

spacecraft—a vehicle that travels in space

star—a large ball of burning gases in space

Sun—the star that the planets move around; the Sun provides light and heat for the planets.

Read More

Orme, Helen, and David Orme. *Let's Explore Jupiter.* Space Launch!
Milwaukee: Gareth Stevens, 2007.

Richardson, Adele. *Jupiter.* First Facts: The Solar System. Mankato,
Minn.: Capstone Press, 2008.

Wimmer, Teresa. *Jupiter.* My First Look at Planets. Mankato, Minn.:
Creative Education, 2007.

Internet Sites

FactHound offers a safe, fun way to find Internet sites related to this
book. All of the sites on FactHound have been researched by our staff.

Here's how:

1. Visit *www.facthound.com*

2. Choose your grade level.

3. Type in this book ID **1429607386**
   for age-appropriate sites. You may also
   browse subjects by clicking on letters,
   or by clicking on pictures and words.

4. Click on the **Fetch It** button.

FactHound will fetch the best sites for you!

Index

Word Count: 131
Grade: 1
Early-Intervention Level: 13

24